THE SANDOE BAG

The SANDOE BAG

A MISCELLANY TO CELEBRATE 50 YEARS

Published by The Cuckoo Press
for John Sandoe (Books) Ltd
10 Blacklands Terrace, London SW3 2SR

© John Sandoe (Books) Ltd 2007

A CIP catalogue reference for this book
is available from the British Library

ISBN 10: 0 9542688 4 9
ISBN 13: 978 0 9542688 4 8

Design and cover illustration by Fenella Willis

Printed and bound in the UK by Antony Rowe Ltd
Bumper's Farm, Chippenham, Wiltshire

'Shopkeepers all the world over don't last long – and never long enough to tell a tale, if there are no customers.'

WILLIAM Y DARLING
The Private Papers of a Bankrupt Bookseller, 1931

.

A BRIEF ACCOUNT
OF THE SHOP AND
ITS INMATES

We are often asked what happened at
10–11 Blacklands Terrace before John
Sandoe's arrival. According to Dirk Bogarde,
No 10 was 'a seedy little newsagent and tobac-
conist' before the war. Picture evidence suggests
that, if seedy, it was at least abundantly stocked.

John tells us that during the war the shop
was occupied by 'a man who sold antiquities to

The shop in the 1930s

popes and people in those big hats'. Downstairs was 'a poodle parlour', the charmingly named Chloe of Chelsea, and upstairs – our paperback room – was a secretarial agency. No 11 was a dress shop: our stock room still has the original mirror on the wall.

Soon after the war, Tom and Ros Chatto took over the ground floor of No 10 as a second-hand bookshop. It was one of several in the immediate area but the Chattos had the advantage of advice and supply from the distinguished antiquarian booksellers Pickering & Chatto, Tom's family firm. Tom was an actor; Ros was – and still is – a theatrical agent. As they pursued their careers, it became increasingly difficult to sustain the bookshop as well, and with the arrival of their second child they decided to trim their operations.

The Chattos' neighbour at No 12 was a vet, Anthony O'Neill. He looked after Churchill's dogs. And he is still there.

John Sandoe opened his shop for business on 11 November 1957. His intention was to offer his own selection of the best current books, and to obtain any other titles he might be asked for – which is what we still try to do today. His grandmother was shocked because he did not

The shop in 1958

have blinds to pull down over the windows on Sundays. We hope that she would forgive us, 50 years on, for opening the door for trade on Sundays.

John grew up and was educated in England. After completing his National Service in the RAF, he went to McGill University in Canada, where he intended to stay because Montreal was more fun than postwar London. He thought about going into publishing, but there was not much of that in Canada then, nor journalism, so he decided to go into trade and open a book-shop. With this in mind he returned to England to learn how to do it properly. Heywood Hill,

3

the Curzon Street bookseller, advised him to speak to J G Wilson at the famous Bumpus Bookshop in Oxford Street, and we're informed

John Sandoe in the 1960s

that he was known as 'the beautiful John' while he worked there.

Before finding premises, John found a colleague, Felicité Gwynn. Soon after leaving her job at J A Allen's horse bookshop she drew his attention to an empty shop next to the vet's where she took her dog. She worked with him

Felicité Gwynn c 1982

from the start, and died in 1986 about three years after retiring. All those who remember her speak of her strong personality and passionate tastes in literature. An unfortunate aspect of the

BBC drama about her sister, Elizabeth David, was that – presumably for the sake of contrast – Felicité was represented as a mousy, servile character. In fact she is vividly recalled not only for her contempt of those she regarded as fools,

but also for her formative influence on clients' reading. 'She loved selling books and was liable to throw them at people on occasion in exasperation,' says John. 'But they would apologise to her, not she to them.'

Customers of a certain age will remember that cigarettes were still sold on the premises when John opened. This was because the shop's cigarette licence was still valid, and its dispensing machine functional, at the end of the Fifties. The only instance of a break-in during John's time was for cigarettes. Now, though we gamely still sport an ashtray (where is it?), tobacco plays a more limited part in our lives. Rumours of associated risks other than burglary have brought it into disrepute. While we don't mind the disrepute, and take a broad view of seediness, we like to think we have a keen instinct for our customers' tastes.

The original bags were black. Before opening, John had asked Katerina Wilczynski (1894–1978) to do a picture of the shop that he could use on writing paper. This was later adapted for use on the bags by one 'MFJ', whose initials appear in the bottom left-hand corner. Alas, the identity

of MFJ has slipped through the net of the staff's collective memory. (Are you out there?)

John sublet the first floor to the secretarial agency for £2/10/- a week, earning a handsome 10 shillings profit from his own £2 rent. In due course the secretaries were ousted in favour of paperbacks and the dress shop next door surrendered to economic pressures. Signatures were exchanged; a hole was made in the wall and RSJs inserted; sliding shelves were put in upstairs. The shop has had the same floor plan ever since.

A curious tale about the sliding shelves emerged later. Around 1990, someone sent us a page from an architectural magazine with an article on Norman Foster's celebrated new law library in Cambridge. It mentioned that the design of the sliding shelves was copied from a little bookshop in Chelsea. A few years later we had a post-prandial visit from a group including a brace of distinguished architects. It was impossible to resist asking Foster if there was any truth in the claim. 'No,' he said bluntly, at which a gentleman in his entourage shifted from one foot to the other and said, 'Well, actually...' Foster turned around and inspected his junior colleague, who evidently had been in charge of bookshelf design on the Cambridge project, then plodded upstairs to see for himself. Nothing more was said but we take it that the story is true.

Until the 1980s, the only other person to work in the shop for a long period was David Cronin, who was here from 1970 until 1979. He returned to New York to sell rare books, but in 1982 he began the public programmes at the New York Public Library. He left in 2000 to become executive director of the New York Council for the Humanities, from which he retired in 2007. Dennis Johnston worked at Sandoe's regularly for some years in the 1970s. James Chatto (Ros's & Tom's elder son) was here for a few months, after which he wrote an excellent short story based on his observations mysteriously entitled 'Tricky Customers' (published in *Winter's Tales*, *New Series 2*, Constable, 1986). Briefer stints were also done by Rachel Stainsby, Candida Brazil, William Morrison-Bell, Charlie Hall and Catherine Hall.

John retired from the bookshop because of ill health in 1989. He says he loved every single day of working here: each morning as he opened the door, right up to the last day on which he gave up the keys, the mere smell of the books delighted him. He now lives in Dorset and

John Sandoe in 2004

Scotland. He rarely comes to London but we frequently send books to him.

The shop was sold to Seán Wyse Jackson, Johnny de Falbe and Stewart Grimshaw – two colleagues and a customer respectively. Letters were sent out to account customers informing them of this change, and also to reassure them that we did not intend to make any changes. This unaccountably confused many people. Eighteen years later, we still get dimly recognised visitors announcing, 'I used to buy all my books with you but I thought you closed down!'

In fact, Sandoe's remains very much as it was in John's day. It looks the same (as we're often fondly told), many of the customers are the same, and there has been remarkable continuity in the staff.

John (Seán) Wyse Jackson started at the shop in 1979. John Sandoe had mentioned to a customer, the novelist Jennifer Johnston, that he needed an extra pair of hands, and when she went home to Ireland she steered Seán onto a boat. It was declared impractical to have two Johns working in the shop and so it fell to the younger one to choose another name. Apart from his annual holiday in Dublin and Kerry, Seán's only known trip abroad in 25 years was to the bookshop Shakespeare & Co in Paris in about 1987. His dedication to Irish literature never flagged. He edited *Myles Before Myles: A Selection of the Earlier Works of Flann O'Brien*; *Aristotle at Afternoon Tea: The Rare Oscar Wilde*; *Flann O'Brien At War: Myles na gCopaleen 1940–1945*; and *James Joyce's Dubliners: An Annotated Edition*. And he co-wrote with Peter Costello a biography of James Joyce's father, *John Stanislaus Joyce*. In 2003, anxious that their

11

children might not grow up to be Irish, he and his wife Ruth decided to leave the UK. They now live in County Wexford, where Seán has written a book about an Englishman of impeccable Irish ancestry, John Lennon: *We All Want to Change the World*.

Johnny de Falbe wandered into the shop looking for work in 1986, a few months after leaving university. Initially he combined selling books with importing ceramics from Kütahya in Turkey, but the books won. There was a moment early on when he nearly ran away to help set up what became Daunt Books, but these cubbyholes in Chelsea are tenacious – and here he is still. He is the author of two novels, *The Glass Night* (1995) and *The Bequest* (2003), and reviews books regularly.

For several years Stewart Grimshaw was in the restaurant business. He owned and ran Provans in the Fulham Road, and later Le Chanterelle. By the mid-1980s he had extracted himself, and on John's retirement he joined Seán and Johnny as a third partner, working part-time. We still have no idea what he does with the other parts (there are many), but those that he puts at our disposal are vastly appreciated. He has a lot of friends, which is understandable because he is

A John Sandoe bag in the Himalayas with, *above*,
customer Robert Binyon and, *below*, some of his porters

The Sandoe bag reaches Uhuru Peak, Kilimanjaro, with
one of our customers – the late, much missed Chris Phillips

terrifically good at dusting. He still maintains that bookshop customers are a joy compared with some he encountered in his restaurants.

Born in Finland, Rubio Lindroos came to London in the early 1970s. He ran a bookshop in Elizabeth Street in Belgravia for several years and then briefly managed one in Covent Garden, specialising in biography. He came to Sandoe's in 1988, and both we and our customers benefited greatly from the formidable range of his reading. He left in 2004 and still lives in London.

Perina Fordham worked part-time in the shop for 14 years, between 1980 and 1994. After leaving us she remarried: she is now Lady Braybrooke, châtelaine of Audley End or one of its outhouses. The stairs (ours, not Audley End's, which accommodate ascent by sedan chair) still tremble from her graceful step. She was a demon with the packing and her international tastes were an example to us all.

It was 1992 when Dan Fenton, a banker who had taken the surprising decision to retire at 26, came to help us out in the shop. To begin with, the bookselling was a sideshow to acting: he took two shows to the Edinburgh Fringe including a hilarious take-off of Loyd Grossman.

Although unorthodox as a sales pitch, it was productive because Mr Grossman became a valued client. Dan, however, abandoned the stage in favour of the shop floor, further demonstrating that Sandoe's is a difficult place to leave. He became a full partner in 1999. It's useful to know that if business is ever slack he can drum up new custom by lampooning celebrities and then slipping them a couple of our catalogues.

Karen Wadman had been a customer for a few years before she started to work at the shop. Her husband was an American banker working in London and she used to hang around shamelessly nagging us for a job. It seemed impossible that she could read as many books as she bought, but soon after she began working here we discovered that she is an insomniac who has read more books than anyone else we know. What's more, she remembers them. It was therefore a blow to our resources when in 2005 she returned to the USA with her husband. Originally from Minnesota, she now lives in Arizona, where we communicate with her frequently.

After 15 years with very few changes, the last four years have brought four new faces.

Ulric van den Bogaerde joined us shortly before Seán left in 2003. We found him feeling

Lama with Sandoe bag, photographed by customer
Lorenzo Ward at the Chamnyay Yeitka Meditation
Centre, Yangon, Myanmar

17

mournful in the Earls Court Road Waterstone's, after some years as a clapper or gaffer or some such thing in the film business. We expect to see a rise in the number of long novels in the 'Favourites' sections of our catalogues because he has just moved to Oxford, from where he will commute to London. He burst into print with his wonderful short story, *An Unexpected Visitor*, which was our 2004 Cuckoo Press pamphlet. He also takes good photographs:

On Rubio's departure we advertised the vacancy in the *Guardian*. A cavalcade of worthies came to see us but we decided in favour of Paul Engles, whose enthusiasm for the written word (and raves) apparently left little time for trivialities such as sleeping or having breakfast. If all goes well he might learn to tie his shoelaces this year, but his fast-growing fan club doesn't much care about this except for his own safety. If occasionally he appears to be abstracted, he might be ruminating on one of his superb poems, a collection of which was published as our 2006 Cuckoo Press pamphlet, *The Goose Who Ate All the Maltesers*.

Like Karen, Heather Hornbeck was a customer who lived round the corner from the shop, married to an American banker. Sherman permitting (Sherman is her dog), we take advantage of her a couple of times a week. Like so many before her, she has found that working in a bookshop does not diminish the book bill.

Some of our most acute customers have realised that we now open on Sundays (from 12 to 6pm). This has been made possible by our newest full-time member of staff, Marzena Pogorzaly. It suits her to work on Sundays so that she has a couple of weekdays on which to attend to her real work: photography. She took this up after her arrival from Gdansk in 1982, and specialises in authors and icebergs. At the time of writing she is in Antarctica, which presumably has more to do with ice than authors, though what she does in her own time is admittedly her business. Whatever else she's doing – swinging from helicopters, discussing aesthetics with Her Majesty's sailors, taking a few pics – she will certainly be finding time to read.

For the last few years, in addition to those on public view there has been a part-time team member doing numerate things in the office upstairs. Caroline Assheton helped us set them rolling. She was followed by Kate Morley, to whom we are grateful for imposing exemplary order on all things, both rolling and stationary, animate and inanimate; which is now admirably maintained by Philippa Spens, whose grandfather, Alan Lennox-Boyd, was (as it happens) present at John's opening party in 1957.

OUR CUSTOMERS

It is commonly said by those who work at John Sandoe's that the best thing about it is the customers. There are exceptions, of course. A few are frightful. We sometimes imagine seating them together at a dinner party and observing the results.

John Sandoe was once heard to say that being a bookseller was a bit like being a GP. The reading habits of bookish people are an intimate part of them, to which we often have more access than those who otherwise know them better. It is a privilege to be familiar with an individual in this way, and often very illuminating. Everyone who has worked at the shop has been appalled, to begin with, to discover how little bibliographic knowledge he or she possesses. Much of what we have learned has been through contact with customers.

We're aware that we have some reputation for having famous customers. It has even been suggested that we put a note on the door saying

Loyd Grossman and the 2007 John Sandoe
50th anniversary bag in Morocco

'Only two celebrities at a time, *please*', but so far this has proved unnecessary. In fact, unlike schoolchildren, this mysterious breed is often not immediately recognisable. Many years ago, while paying for a novel by Anita Brookner, a man informed us with excitement that at a dinner party the previous evening he had been sitting beside someone who had actually met her. He remained unaware that Dr Brookner was standing beside him.

You would think anyone would recognise Elton John but it isn't quite true: he once watched with delight as a celebrated Knightsbridge interior decorator cut across him, with a voice like a choir of corncrakes, in praise of Roy Strong's diaries. 'It's bitch, bitch, bitch!' she declared with glee. 'I'll have three of the old queen's filth, please,' Sir Elton requested discreetly after her departure.

Shirley Hazzard might not be a name that sells copies of *Hello!*, but her single visit to us remains legendary for having made half the staff present swoon in awe – which is perhaps why she has never returned.

Speaking of that august magazine, a paparazzo managed to catch Gwyneth Paltrow leaving us with a Sandoe bag containing an expensive cookery book. The caption accused her of meanness for going to a second-hand shop. We haven't seen her since either, but if anyone reading this knows her then please convey our best wishes and tell her that we too felt rather offended.

The last name we'll drop is John Betjeman. Still hanging from one of the bookshelves in the shop is this cardboard cut-out, on which the poet himself drew a monocle because he said it made him look just like the novelist Radclyffe Hall.

Customers have sent us many missives over the years, of which a sprinkling has been fondly preserved. Of those that are printable, our favourite remains this one from Robert Conn.

THE JOHN SANDOE POST A BOOK TEAM

When Robert Lister gets bored on his holidays, he sends us a quiz. We received this from him in 1998 from Morocco:

'He lacked that combination of relentless ambition, superhuman energy and boundless self-confidence that had distinguished his father – which is probably as good a definition of greatness as any other.' £10.99

'I think that when in 1 Cor vii 25 St Paul says he has "no commandment from the Lord concerning virgins" we must not be tempted to say that virgins are fortunate indeed.' £17.50

'To laugh often and much; to win the respect of intelligent people and the affection of children; to earn the appreciation of honest critics and the betrayal of false friends; to know even one life has breathed easier because you lived. This is to have succeeded.' £4.95

Robert promises a second bottle of champagne (the first was duly won, and drunk: it was a quiet day) to the first person who can tell us where these quotations come from.

We regularly send books to CB Thompson in Patmos. We have strict instructions to wrap them first in plastic bags, in case the postman drops the packages in the sea. He also asks us to write the addresses in capital letters, which we hope is a reflection of his postman's eyesight rather than our penmanship. Sometimes he sends us postcards and photographs. The explanation on the back of the gem opposite reads:

And, after a ravishing fortnight in Athens for The Games, why not spend a relaxing few days in Patmos, jewel of the Dodekanese, renowned for its airy tourist appointments...? (A photo taken about a week ago. I do not expect that the tourists visiting the beach this summer will find a repaired Seat of Easement. Because in the past they had recourse to the field 200yds from the house, I painted the rock wall with DANGER! SNAKES! It was successful.)

Sad to say, it is not unknown for a customer's cheque to emerge after many years from a cranny in our well-ordered office. Even so, this thoughtful letter, which arrived with its faded enclosures in October 2001, took us all by surprise:

Gentlemen
Going through old papers recently, I found the enclosed invoice and money order which I forward without further delay. Before I moved to Canada I

lived in Chelsea and first met John Sandoe when he opened his bookshop. After all this time I can but assume he let me have these two books when I was visiting London, I suppose in 1978. All I can do now is to apologise. I have no idea how these papers became so mislaid. None the less, I hope the shop continues to flourish.
Yours truly,
John Johnston

We accept Mr Johnston's gracious apology and assure him that the shop does indeed continue to flourish – thanks, in part, to recent tightening of our credit terms.

Dr Sabri Challah in Marrakesh

THE BOOK TRADE

When John Sandoe retired in 1989 it was the heyday of Waterstone's, and independent bookshops were said to be in the doldrums. Publishers' London trade counters had gone and they were cutting back on reps. When ordering books, we sent postcards or had to spell the details down the phone to someone struggling with a new-fangled computer at a warehouse in the Midlands. 'P–i–c–a–s–s–o, yes, he's an artist, you have just published a biography of him.' It was dispiriting.

We soon introduced a computer for customer accounts but it still seemed – incredibly, in retrospect – that computers would otherwise remain unnecessary to us. That changed when bibliographic data stopped being produced in the big red directories and transferred, after a brief and dreadful phase with microfiche, to CD-ROM.

Assuming our sympathy because of our old-fashioned appearance, the more Luddite of our customers used to be quick to praise us for not doing everything on computer. But we had more computers lurking upstairs than they realised. Ironically, we had difficulty in the 1990s because the software we needed to access books globally was not available. The technology has since caught up with our needs, which enables us to continue doing what we do best: supplying a broad range of good books to our customers.

The book trade underwent an important change in the mid-1990s with the collapse of the Net Book Agreement. This had been an agreement between book publishers that prices should be fixed, on the grounds that it was in the public interest. Pressure was brought by retailers wishing to discount, and the Office of Fair Trading argued that price maintenance was no longer beneficial. Large publishers, anxious to please the retail chains, were not prepared to defend it, and the public's case was made by a tiny number of small publishers, whom we supported vigorously. The case was lost and – as predicted – while a few books have come down in price, the range of backlist titles available has suffered and their prices have increased.

It is a measure of how fast things have changed that internet bookselling was scarcely

ODESSA

SEVASTOPOL

Above Mr and Mrs Alan Ogden take us to new markets.
Below This is Caroline Assheton. The background may
suggest a flooded quarry in Hertfordshire but she claims
that she and the bag went to the Galapagos

referred to in the NBA case. And while the agreement's demise appears to have opened the way for Amazon in the UK, the fact is that it would have been rendered absurd by the arrival of books from Amazon in the US, who were not governed by the NBA.

We are regularly asked if we're affected by Amazon – some people express frank astonishment that we're still in business. But some independent bookshops who survived the 1990s are thriving. In our case this is not through discounting, which would be a waste of time because we couldn't be competitive, but by working hard to do what we always did: selecting books, making suggestions when invited, providing a service. In this respect, the internet is a gift to us as it is to everyone else, not a threat. We too sell books via our website.

CATALOGUES AND
PUBLICATIONS

Besides doing our best to be efficient, we regard the discerning selection of books as integral to our survival. This is a two-way process: it's partly responding to what our customers like, and partly conveying our own tastes. If we sometimes appear to have a very specialised new book in the window, it will either have been bought because we know of one or two customers who might be interested in it or because one of us cares about it. We like to think that we know why every book on our shelves is there: not that we have read them all, as some people fondly imagine, but that we have an inkling of why this or that might be the book for someone to read on a given subject. The clearest form for this selection process is our catalogues.

Until 1989 the shop produced just one catalogue a year, for Christmas. Since then we have done interim lists every three months. This involves trawling through publishers' catalogues, talking with reps, reading or glancing through

Our former colleague Karen Wadman takes the
word to the Arizona desert

proofs, following up hearsay. Although dependent on 'feeds', we like to consider for ourselves what we've been fed before recommending it to anyone else, for this is what independence in bookselling means. Sometimes we miss books that should evidently have been in our lists because we were never told about them, which is frustrating. These may surface in the 'Recent Favourites' section of a subsequent list, where we round up a few books that our staff have enjoyed lately. The selection usually includes some long-in-the-tooth classics, but the inclusion of recent titles usually reflects our sense that they have not had the currency they deserve.

Besides giving out our lists in the shop, we send them all over the world to account customers as well as posting them on our website. Of course, we're aware that we're not the sole distributors of the books we list, and anyone could easily get most of them from another bookshop or online. Occasionally we even get phoned by apologetic booksellers asking how to get a title that a customer is jabbing at on one of our lists. And if booksellers also sometimes avail themselves of our work, then we should feel pleased that the books get a further airing, and remind ourselves that the process of making and articulating our suggestions can only benefit the service we try to provide.

Some – but surprisingly few – customers have observed, on scanning the front of our Christmas Books lists, that every year for the last decade or so we have produced a little pamphlet, which can be claimed free with any order from the catalogue. They are all written either by a member of staff or a customer, and they are produced under the imprint of The Cuckoo Press, which was the name used when publishing Johnny's first novel. Like *The Glass Night*, they are designed and sub-edited by Fenella Willis, Johnny's wife, who also did our lovely bookmarks. She has now produced 12 of them (13 including the one you are holding), and they amount to an exquisite, distinctive set of little books of which we are very proud. They are:

1995: *The Foible of Aristide Apple* (John de Falbe)★
1996: *Phenolphthalein: A Fictional Quest for the Eighth Plot* (John Wyse Jackson)
1997: *'Visions Fugitives'* (William Boyd)★
1998: *The Quest for Lavishes Ghast* (Muriel Spark)★
1999: *Gualta* (Javier Marías)★
2000: *The Beast* (Michael Krüger)
2001: *Love's Lesson* (Edna O'Brien)★
2002: *Toodles Made the War Worthwhile* (Arabella Boxer)
2003: *A Disgraceful Anomaly* (Julian Mitchell)
2004: *An Unexpected Visitor* (Ulric van den Bogaerde)
2005: *My Dog Ian* (Philip Hensher)
2006: *The Goose Who Ate all the Maltesers* (Paul Engels)

★Copies still available at time of going to press

Sandoe's 2007: customer Adrian Noskwith, *far left*, with, *from left*, Dan Fenton, Ulric van den Bogaerde and Johnny de Falbe

The staff at John Sandoe's, past and present, thank all our customers for their loyal support and friendship during the last half-century. We look forward to continuing to provide you all with books, and trust that our successors will enjoy doing the same for your descendants.